TABLE OF CONTENTS

CHAPTER 1

TROUBLE IN TEXAS

In 1832, Texas was part of Mexico. The Mexican government thought too many Americans were in Texas. These Americans were called Texians. Mexico **enforced** new, unfair laws on them. The Texians wanted freedom. They would start a **revolution**.

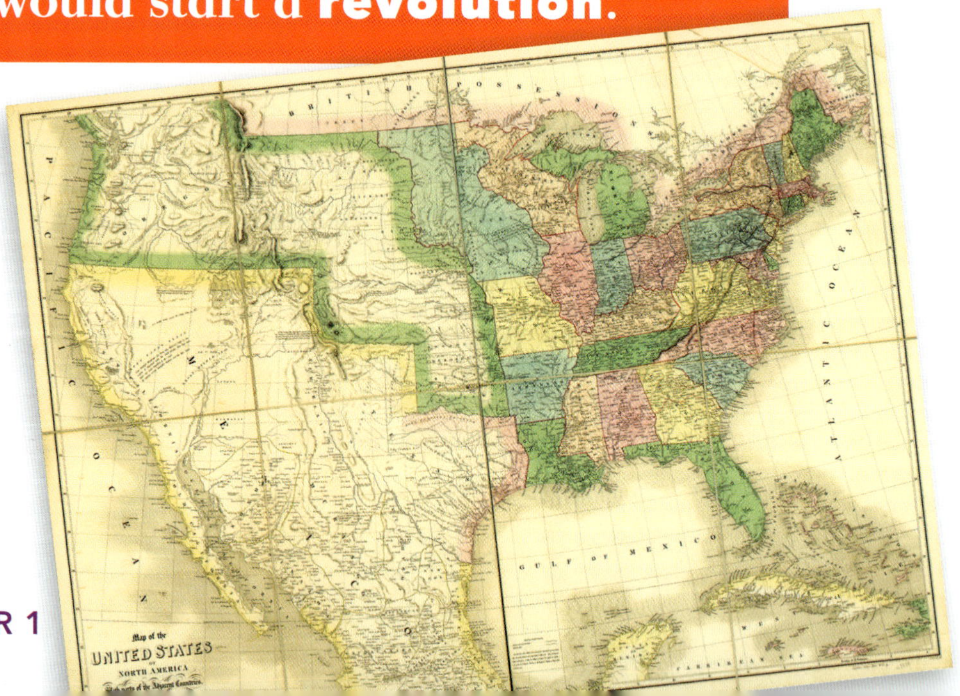

TURNING POINTS IN U.S. HISTORY

TEXAS REVOLUTION

by Christopher Forest

pogo

Ideas for Parents and Teachers

Pogo Books let children practice reading informational text while introducing them to nonfiction features such as headings, labels, sidebars, maps, and diagrams, as well as a table of contents, glossary, and index.

Carefully leveled text with a strong photo match offers early fluent readers the support they need to succeed.

Before Reading

- "Walk" through the book and point out the various nonfiction features. Ask the student what purpose each feature serves.
- Look at the glossary together. Read and discuss the words.

Read the Book

- Have the child read the book independently.
- Invite him or her to list questions that arise from reading.

After Reading

- Discuss the child's questions. Talk about how he or she might find answers to those questions.
- Prompt the child to think more. Ask: The Texians fought for independence. Can you think of other times when people have fought for independence?

Pogo Books are published by Jump!
5357 Penn Avenue South
Minneapolis, MN 55419
www.jumplibrary.com

Library of Congress Cataloging-in-Publication Data

Names: Forest, Christopher, author.
Title: Texas Revolution / by Christopher Forest.
Description: Minneapolis, MN: Pogo Books, [2021]
Series: Turning points in U.S. history | Includes index.
Audience: Ages 7-10 | Audience: Grades 2-3
Identifiers: LCCN 2019046359 (print)
LCCN 2019046360 (ebook)
ISBN 9781645274377 (hardcover)
ISBN 9781645274384 (paperback)
ISBN 9781645274391 (ebook)
Subjects: LCSH: Texas–History–Revolution, 1835-1836
Juvenile literature.
Classification: LCC F390 .F695 2021 (print)
LCC F390 (ebook) | DDC 976.4/03–dc23
LC record available at https://lccn.loc.gov/2019046359
LC ebook record available at
https://lccn.loc.gov/2019046360

Editor: Jenna Gleisner
Designer: Jenna Casura

Photo Credits: Kean Collection/Getty, cover; Sean Pavone/Shutterstock, 1, 9, 20-21; railway fx/Shutterstock, 3; Library of Congress, 4, 8; North Wind Picture Archives/Alamy, 5; The Picture Art Collection/Alamy, 6-7; ClassicStock/Alamy, 10-11; Everett Collection Historical/Alamy, 12-13; World History Archive, 14-15; Archive Images/Alamy, 16; Universal History Archive/Getty, 17; DEA Picture Library/Getty, 18-19; Zurinzulkan/Shutterstock, 23.

Printed in the United States of America at Corporate Graphics in North Mankato, Minnesota.

Native Americans first lived in Texas. Spanish **explorers** arrived there in the 1500s. They **claimed** the land for Spain. Spain controlled Texas and Mexico for many years.

Mexico won **independence** in 1821. In 1833, the country got a new **president**. His name was Antonio López de Santa Anna. He was an army **general**.

WHAT DO YOU THINK?

Santa Anna was a war hero in Mexico. This helped him become president. Do you think a general would make a good president? Why or why not?

Antonio López
de Santa Anna

CHAPTER 2

BATTLES BEGIN

Many Texians did not support Santa Anna. Santa Anna wanted to control them. They wanted independence.

Texians in the city of Gonzales had a cannon. Santa Anna wanted it. He sent his army to get it in October 1835. The Texians fought back. They won.

In December 1835, Texians took over the Alamo. It was a **fort**. It had been under Mexican control. The Texians refused to leave it. Santa Anna sent his army to take the fort back. He demanded the Texians **surrender**.

The Texians did not. They fought. The Battle of the Alamo lasted 13 days. Mexico won.

DID YOU KNOW?

Davy Crockett was a **pioneer**. He had explored the United States. He fought at the Alamo. He lost his life.

Davy Crockett

Sam Houston

The Battle of Coleto took place just weeks later. The Texians lost. The Mexicans captured some Texians. They said they would bring them to prison. Instead, they killed them. The event became known as the Goliad **Massacre**.

Other Texians heard what happened. They grew angry. They formed a large army. Sam Houston led them.

On April 21, 1836, Houston's army arrived at the San Jacinto River. They surrounded the Mexican army. Santa Anna had to surrender. The war was over. It had lasted six months. Texas was free.

Battle of San Jacinto

TAKE A LOOK!

Take a look at this map. Which battles did Mexico win? Which did Texians win?

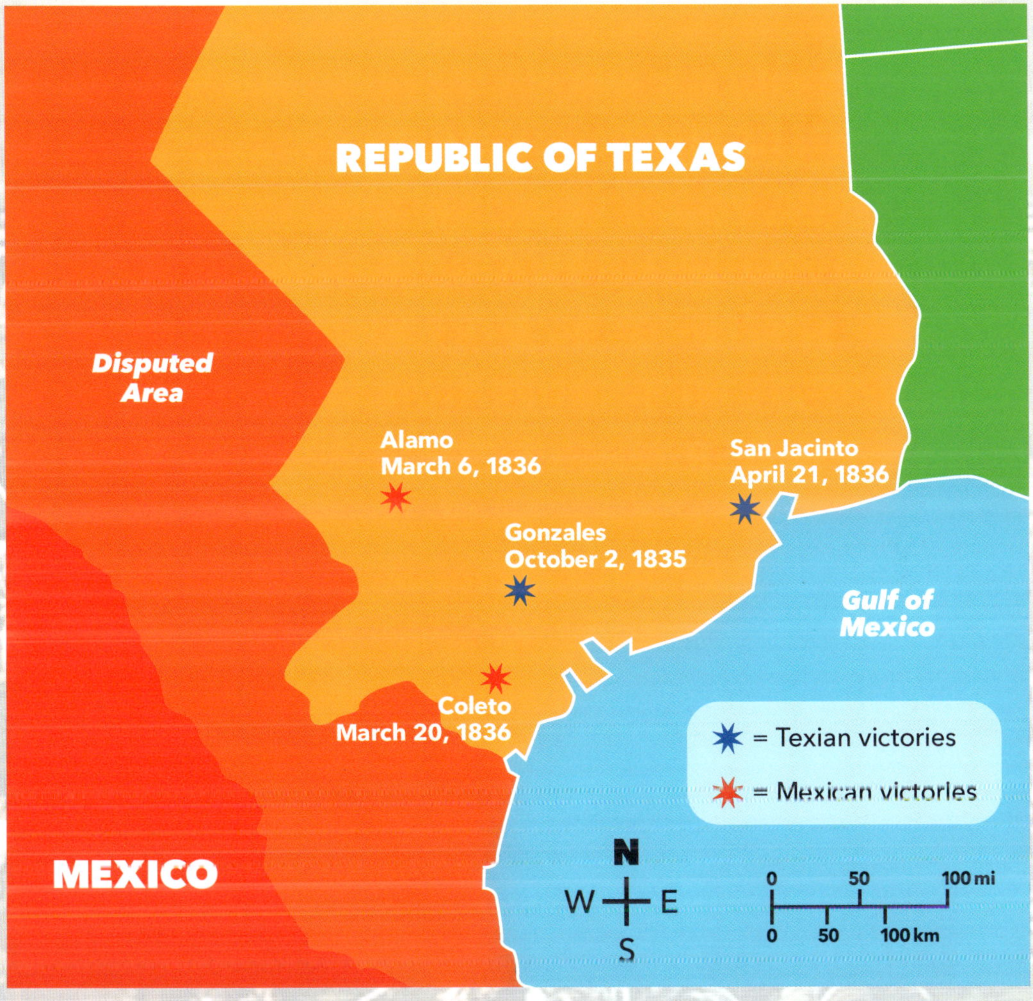

CHAPTER 3

TEXAS IS FREE

Texas **declared** itself a free country. Houston became its president. Some Texians wanted to join the United States. The United States **annexed** Texas. It became a state in 1845.

Sam Houston

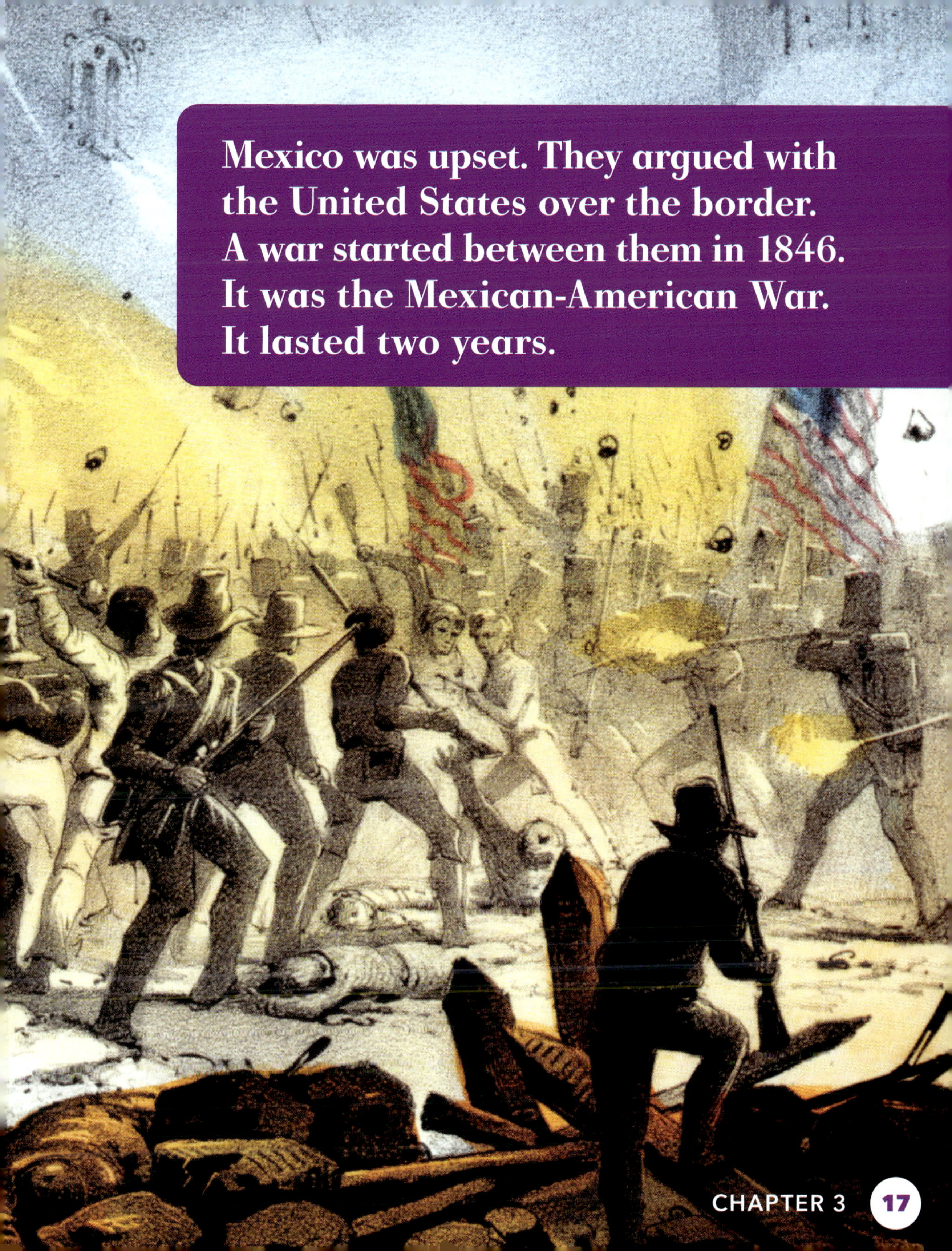

Mexico was upset. They argued with the United States over the border. A war started between them in 1846. It was the Mexican-American War. It lasted two years.

The United States won and kept Texas. They got more land, too. That area would become many states. These include New Mexico, Utah, Nevada, Arizona, California, and Colorado.

WHAT DO YOU THINK?

Texas was once its own country. Hawaii, Vermont, and California were, too. Do you live in one of these states? What do you think it would be like if it were a country instead?

San Antonio

The Texas Revolution changed the country forever. Texas left Mexico. The United States gained new land. Is your state part of the country because of the Texas Revolution?

QUICK FACTS & TOOLS

TIMELINE

1718
Spain founds the city of San Antonio, Texas.

1821
Mexico gains freedom from Spain.

1835
The Texas Revolution begins. The Battle of Goliad occurs. Texians take over the city of San Antonio.

1836
The Battles of the Alamo, Coleto, and San Jacinto take place. The Texas Revolution ends. Texas becomes a country.

1845
Texas joins the United States in December.

1846
The Mexican-American War begins.

1848
The Mexican-American War ends. The border between Mexico and the United State extends to the Rio Grande River. The area that is now New Mexico, Utah, Nevada, Arizona, California, and part of Colorado becomes part of the United States.

GLOSSARY

annexed: Added to a country so as to become a part of it.

claimed: Took land for another country.

declared: Made known in an official way.

enforced: Made sure a law or rule was followed.

explorers: People who travel and look around in order to discover things.

fort: A building where soldiers live.

general: A person in charge of an army.

independence: The time when a country gains freedom from outside control.

massacre: An event where many people die in a cruel way.

pioneer: A person who explores territories and settles there.

president: The leader of a country.

revolution: A violent overthrow of a country's government or ruler by the people who live there.

surrender: To give up.

INDEX

TO LEARN MORE

Finding more information is as easy as 1, 2, 3.

1. Go to www.factsurfer.com
2. Enter "TexasRevolution" into the search box.
3. Choose your book to see a list of websites.

FACT SURFER